395.1
Pit

Pitt, Valerie

AUTHOR

Let's Find Out About Manners

TITLE

DATE DUE	BORROWER'S NAME	ROOM NUMBER

395.1
Pit

Pitt, Valerie

Let's Find Out About Manners

let's
find out
about
manners

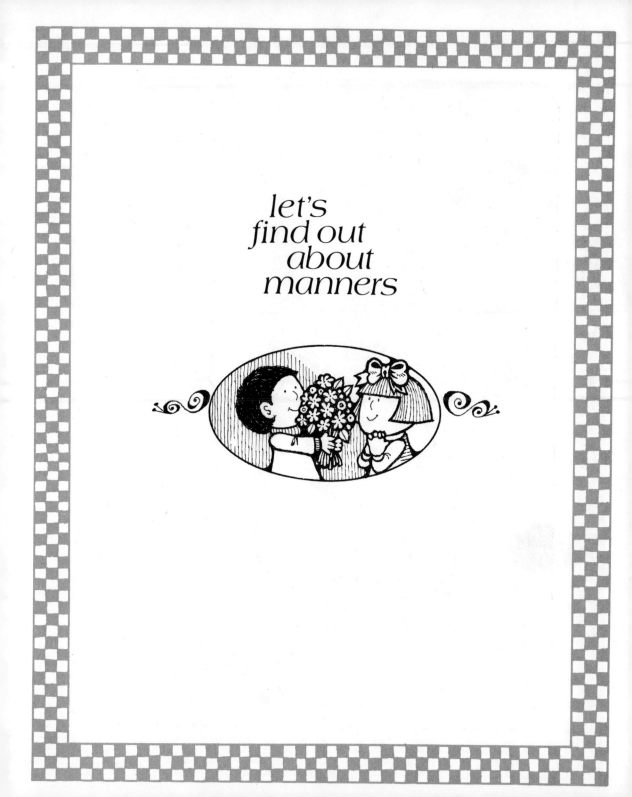

let's find out about manners

by valerie pitt

pictures by olivia h.h. cole

FRANKLIN WATTS | NEW YORK | LONDON

See page 32 for Library of Congress
Cataloging in Publication Data

Copyright © 1972 by Franklin Watts, Inc.
Printed in the United States of America

4

Have you ever seen young puppies feeding out
of a dish?
Each one pushes and scuffles and tries to nose
the other puppies away from the food.
The smaller puppies may end up with only a
few mouthfuls.
The biggest, strongest puppies will get most of
the food for themselves.

Suppose people acted like animals.

Your birthday party would be a sad affair.

Jimmy, the tallest, would reach over and eat
most of the ice cream and would splatter the
rest in your face.

Susie, who is greedy and selfish, would stuff all
the little chocolate cakes into her pocket and
rush home to gobble them.

Steven, who is big and strong, might shove
everyone away from the hot dogs and grab
them all for himself.

The other guests might not even get a single
cookie to eat.

What a miserable party it would be.

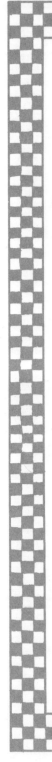

Luckily there is a difference in the way animals
and people behave.

From the time we were babies and grabbed
everything that looked or smelled or felt good
to us, we have been taught manners.

Manners are polite ways of behaving.

Manners are based on thoughtfulness for others.

They help make it possible for all of us to live
together—whether we are old or young, strong
or weak—without fighting among ourselves.

Manners make living with other people more
comfortable and pleasant.

At home, everyone in the family will be happier
if you say "please" and "thank you" and do
not just grab for things.

At school, you will get along better if you are
thoughtful toward your teacher and your
classmates.

In a store, the clerk will be more helpful if you
ask politely, "Do you have a red frisbee,
please, sir?" instead of mumbling, "I wanna
red frisbee."

On the bus, people will be pleased to see you
give your seat to a lady who is struggling with
a lot of packages. And the lady will be grateful
because you have made her day easier.

Even primitive tribes have rules of behavior.
If you are a stranger and break one of the
tribe's important rules by mistake, they may
even kill you.
Of course, that is not going to happen here.
If you are impolite, people will just notice it
and may even tell you how rude you are.
It is often the people with good manners who
are liked the most and who are the most fun
to be with.
Of course, if you live alone, there is no one to
see you if you pile food into your mouth,
pick your nose, or leave all your clothes
in a heap on the floor.
But if you are with other people, those habits
will not make you very popular.

Pretend you have two friends called Jackie and
  Tim.

Jackie walks into your house without knocking.

She picks up an apple without asking and chews
  it with her mouth open like a human washing
  machine.

When your mother is not looking, Jackie kicks
  the cat and walks out with one of your books
  under her arm.

Tim knocks on the door and waits for you to
ask him inside.

He waits for your mother to ask if he would like
an apple.

He chews it with his mouth closed.

If he does not like your cat, he just ignores it.

He asks if he may please borrow your book,
saying he will take care of it and return it
soon.

When he leaves, he thanks your mother for
having him in.

Which friend is more fun to be with—Jackie
or Tim?

Who has better manners?

Sometimes rules of behavior are called etiquette.
Etiquette is the correct way of doing something.
If you want to write a letter to your
  congressman, a book of etiquette will tell you
  how to address him correctly.
There are rules of etiquette for all occasions,
  from eating soup to giving a grand ball.
But all those rules are based on one idea: what
  makes things easier and more pleasant for
  everyone.

Suppose you are invited to a friend's house for
   dinner.

If you do any of the following things, you will
   not be making things pleasant for your
   friend's family.

—Going to the table with dirty hands or face.

—Starting to eat before everyone else.

—Saying "ugh" and shoving the plate aside if
   you do not like the food.

—Stretching across the table for the salt and
   pepper instead of asking someone to please
   pass them to you.

—Speaking with your mouth full.

—Waving your knife and fork around like
   windmills.

—Leaving the table before everyone is finished,
   unless you have been told you may.

Politeness, or lack of it, shows in almost
 everything you do.

It even "shows" on the telephone.

When you make a call, the polite thing to do is
 state your name straight away, like this:

"Hello, this is Mary Johnson. May I speak to
 Patsy, please?"

If someone telephones your house and asks to
 speak to your mother, the polite thing to say
 is, "Just a moment, please," before you go to
 call her.

Most rules of etiquette have good reasons
behind them.

Do you know why people first started shaking
hands when they met?

Many years ago, men carried swords.

If a man put out his hand, it showed he was not
going to use his sword.

Today, we still shake hands as a sign of
friendship.

Special respect is shown to elderly people.

This is because they have lived longer and have
perhaps gained more wisdom, and because
they may be frail.

You can show respect by giving up your seat to
an elderly person and by addressing him or
her politely as "sir" or "ma'am."

Etiquette is different from country to country.

In America we do not always say "Good
morning" to the shopkeeper when we arrive
to shop.

But in France we would be considered very
rude if we did not say "Bonjour" ("Good
morning") as we entered the shop.

In America we keep our shoes on when we
enter a friend's house.

If we were in Japan, we would take them off
so as not to damage the delicate straw mats
on the floor.

No matter what country you are in, there is
really only one rule to learn for good
manners.
It is often called the Golden Rule. It is this:
Behave in the sort of way you would like
other people to behave to you.

Would you like someone to interrupt, every
time you started to speak?
Or ask you why you have such big ears?
Or break all your crayons just when you have
them all pointed at the ends?

When you think of it like that, manners make
    a lot of sense.
If you remember how you would like people
    to behave to you, you will find that you will
    behave that way to other people.
You will have learned the most important thing
    about good manners.

ABOUT THE AUTHOR

Valerie Pitt was born and educated in England, and received a diploma in journalism from London Polytechnic. She has been a reporter on an English newspaper, a beauty and fashion writer on an English weekly magazine, and assistant fashion editor for *Woman's Own*, a magazine with a large circulation in England. She has traveled extensively in Europe and the United States and has covered the couture collections in Florence and Rome. After having lived for some time in the United States, she now makes her home in London.

Among the books she has written are *Let's Find Out About the City*, *Let's Find Out About Names, Let's Find Out About Clothes, Let's Find Out About Neighbors,* and *Let's Find Out About the Family*.

ABOUT THE ARTIST

Olivia H. H. Cole, born and raised in New York City, attended the High School of Music and Art and later Pratt Institute. She has won a number of awards including the AIGA, Chicago Book Clinic and Society of Illustrators. She is a member of the Society of Illustrators.

Library of Congress Cataloging in Publication Data

Pitt, Valerie.
    Let's find out about manners.

    SUMMARY: Discusses the basic, commonsense reasons behind everyday rules of etiquette.
    1. Etiquette for children and youth. [1. Etiquette] I. Cole, Olivia H. H., illus. II. Title.
BJ1843.C5P57   395'.1'22   70-183898
ISBN 0-531-00082-6